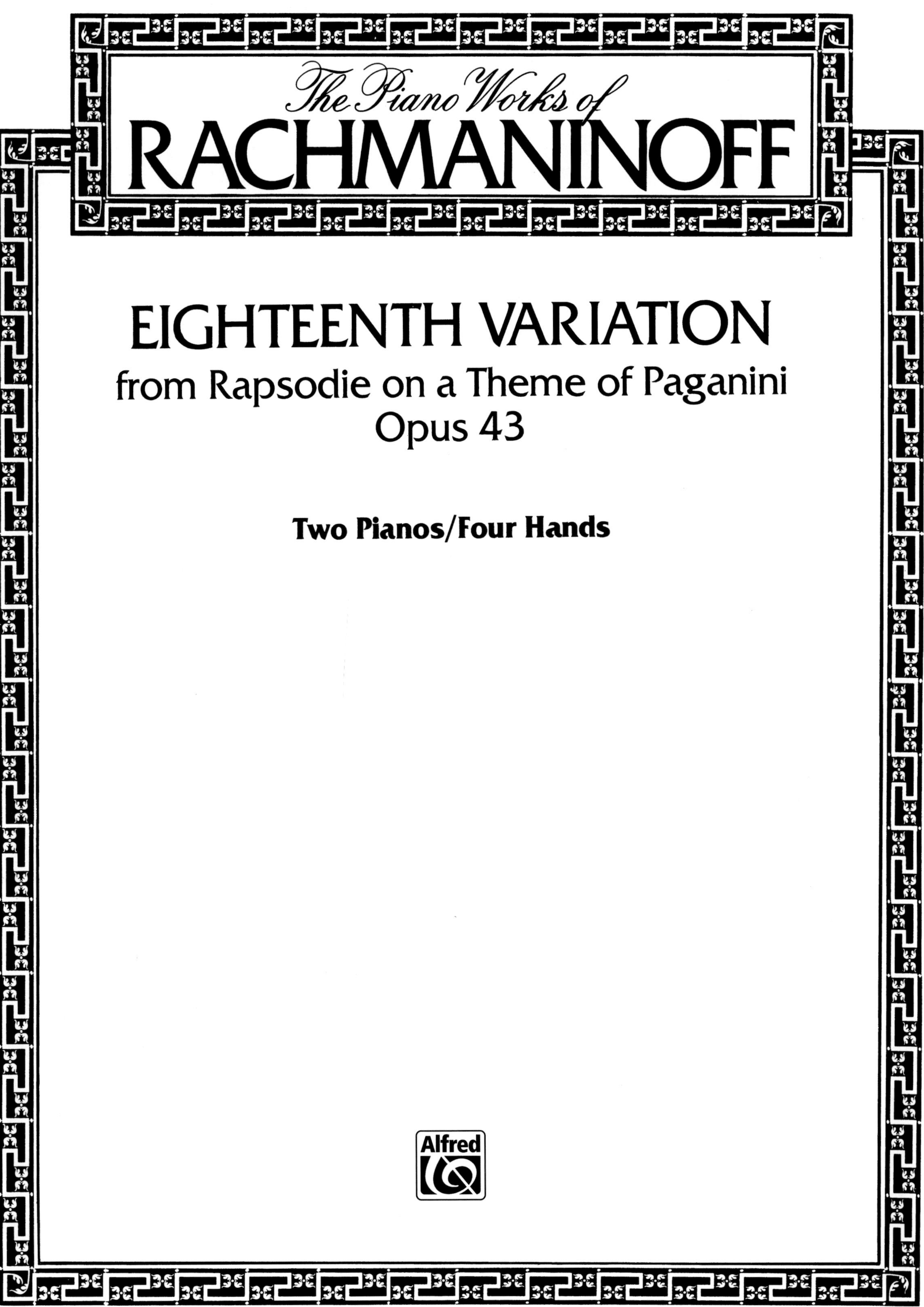

The Piano Works of
RACHMANINOFF

EIGHTEENTH VARIATION
from Rapsodie on a Theme of Paganini
Opus 43

Two Pianos/Four Hands

Alfred

Eighteenth Variation
From Rapsodie on a Theme of Paganini
Op. 43
S. RACHMANINOFF
Andante cantabile
pp
mf
p
I
II
mf
dim.
p
I
II
cresc.
I
II

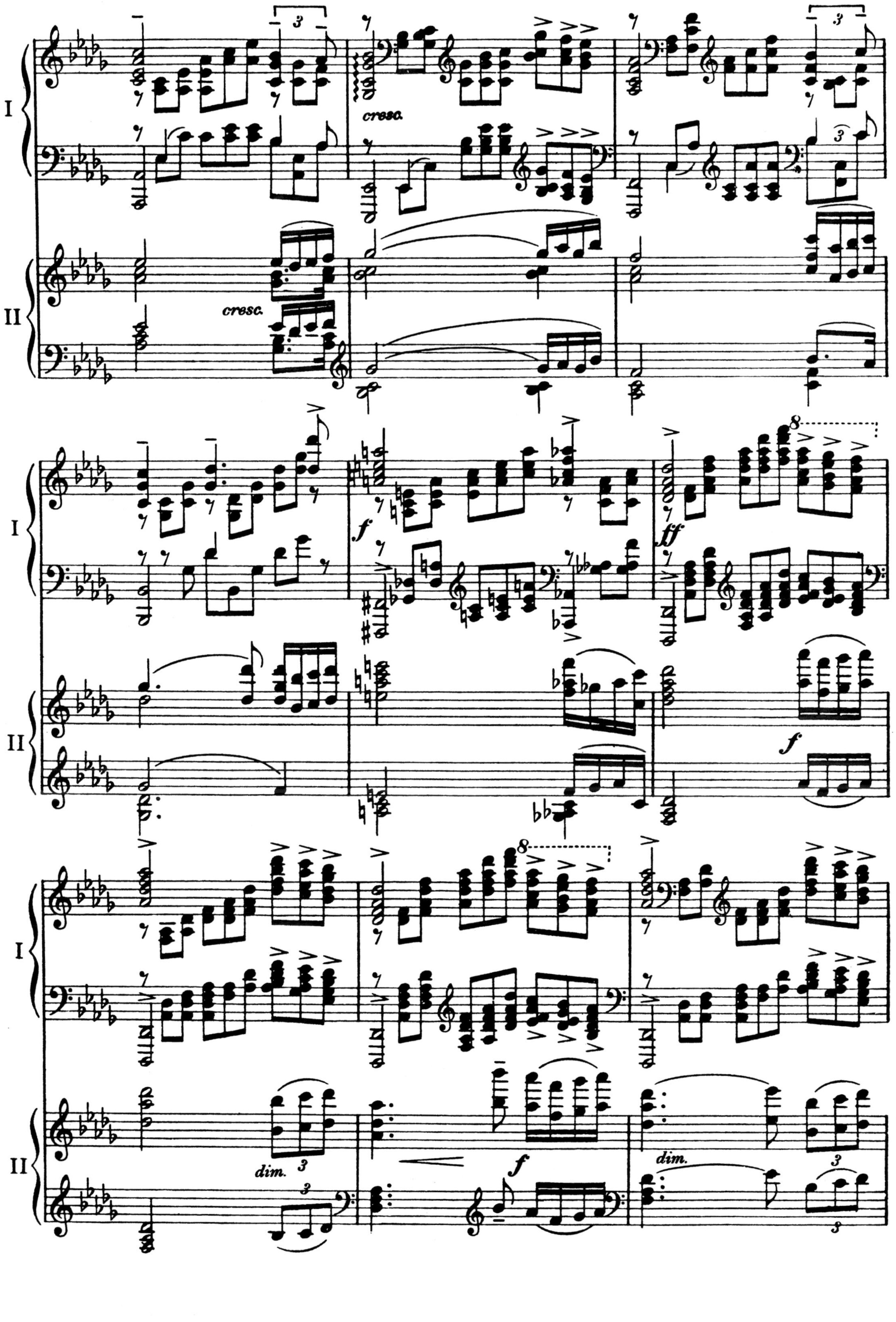
I
II
cresc.
cresc.
f
ff
f
dim.
f
dim.

p
dim.
rit.
pp
3
3
I
II

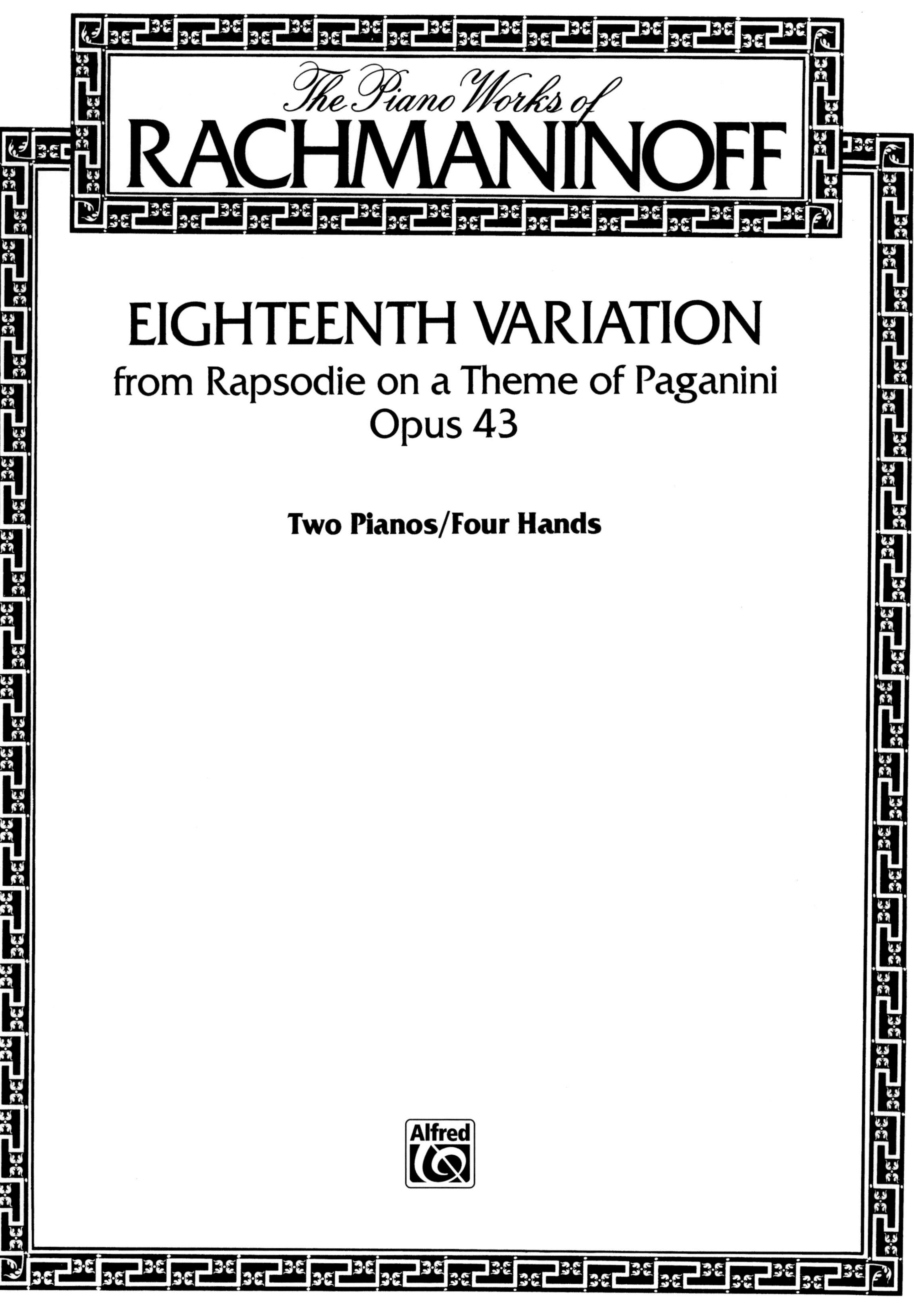

The Piano Works of
RACHMANINOFF

EIGHTEENTH VARIATION
from Rapsodie on a Theme of Paganini
Opus 43

Two Pianos/Four Hands

Alfred

Eighteenth Variation
From Rapsodie on a Theme of Paganini
Op. 43

S. RACHMANINOFF

5
I
II
dim.
mf
3
3
p dolce
I
II
3
dim.
mf
dim.
p
3
3
dim.
3
pp

p
dim.
rit.
pp
I
II

AF380144